When The Mouse Became The Lion

Salina

Copyright © 2024

by Salina. All rights reserved. Printed in Australia. No part of this book may be used or reproduced in any manner whatsoever without written permission except in the case of reprints in the context of reviews.

ISBN:

Paperback: 978-1-7635050-0-1
Ebiook: 978-1-7635050-1-8

For Gigi,
My little lion.

Contents

An act of war… 1

Anger, Frustration, Hurt. 5
   GAME OVER 6
   Once burned, twice shy 8
   Unsafe 9
   Thank-you 10
   Chasey 11
   Whatever I Want 12
   Injustice 13
   Hypocrisy 14
   Rules of the game 16
   What women face when they chase their dreams … 17
   Feigned Ignorance 18
   Unwanted Admiration 19
   Sexualisation 20
   Silenced 21
   More Than a Body 22
   Invisible 23
   Family Bonds 24
   Reflections of a Feminist 25
   Rage 26
   Hurt 27
   Fake Apologies 28
   Refuge 29
   Approval 30
   Expectations 31
   The torture of insomnia 32
   Feminism 33
   Things I was told growing up that would make me a slut 34
   Generational Abuse 35
   Insomnia 36
   Welcome to 2022 37
   The Parent Trap 38
   Anxiety 39
   Dark Cloud 40

Hope, Strength, Healing.   41

Soul GPS   42
Moon Woman   43
Stardust   44
Bow Down   45
Decisions   46
Magical   47
Watched   48
Alive   49
Recovering People Pleaser   50
Energy   51
Awakening   52
Body Map   53
Take Up Space   54
Wild   55
Opinionated Woman   56
I can spend my cash how I want   58
On acceptance of others   59
A conversation with my younger self   60
The crazy one   63
What trauma looks like to me   64
Ignored   66
Breaking Cycles   67
Liquid Gold   68
The power of silence   69
Honouring my knowing   70
Belonging   72
Voices   73
When a loved one is in an abusive relationship   74
His Actions   76
The Controller   77
When Generations Collide   78
The Darkness Within   79
Walls   80
Daily Renewal   81
Look Within   82
Bewitched   83

Cut the cord	84
You …	85
Sisterhood	86
Stranger to myself	87
Universe	88
Ancestral Messages	89
The Real Me	90
Freedom	92

Love, Connection, Relationships. — 93

Sister	94
Full	95
What If?	96
Dear Mama	98
The force of love	99
Stranger in my bed	100
Parental Tension of Opposites	101
To My Daughter	102
Motherhood	103
Bluebird	104
Tina/ Mothers of immigrants	105
Single Parents	106
What I'm going to teach my daughter …	107
Pure Love	108
Naked	109

Thoughts, Opinions, Learnings. — 111

Impact	112
Judgement	113
My Perfect Day	114
R.E.S.P.E.C.T (what it means to me)	115
Question	116
Hypothesis	117
What I Keep Hidden	118
Autumn Leaves	119
Bitter People	120
About the Author	123

"When a woman finally learns that pleasing the world is impossible, she becomes free to learn how to please herself."

~ Glennon Doyle
Untamed

An act of war…

By publishing this book, I am committing an act of war in my culture.

A 'good Wog girl' remains silent.

This book is a missile aimed at breaking down the outdated elements of my culture so as to make room for more of the amazing parts.

I was born in Australia to a second-generation Italian mother, and a first-generation Greek father. We are considered 'Wogs'… which is what Australian's call anyone with a European heritage. I imagine the 'Wog' culture would be the same as any European immigrant family living elsewhere, (like the U.S.A and U.K for example).

I started life as an outsider, everywhere. I was not an 'Aussie' at home, and when I travelled to Italy and Greece, I discovered I wasn't an Italian or a Greek either.

Us Wogs live in no (wo)man's land and this has created a special type of culture.

Here's my take on it…

Our grandparents (or parents) came to Australia (or the U.S.A, or U.K) for a better life. When they left their countries, they not only brought with them their belongings (as little as they had), but they also brought their culture and 'way of life'.

Surrounded by strangers and unfamiliar customs, they clung to their culture like a life raft in dangerous seas. But what they clung to was not their culture in its purest form; it was just a snapshot of it.

Culture is constantly evolving and changing. As our grandparents (or parents) were no longer in Italy or Greece (or Macedonia…etc.) to see these changes happening, they retained what they had once known of their culture – their way of doing things, frozen in time.

This was the birth of the 'Wog' culture, and it hasn't changed since.

There is so much to love about this culture, and I admit I may have gone through a phase of exaggerating my 'Wogness' during my teens. There is the sense of community and the importance of family (which can also be a challenge ... I write about this in my poems). There's the amazing food, the parties, the traditions and loyalty. The sense of 'togetherness'.

But there is also a darker side to the 'Wog' culture, and in this woke world, I think it's time we addressed it. Generation after generation, NOTHING has changed. While most of the world is moving along at lightning pace, it's almost as if the Wog culture is a small-town community trapped in time and space.

Yes, I am aware there are many such cultures around the world still clinging to old-fashioned views like the ones I talk about below. I can only talk from the perspective of my own culture, but if you come from a different culture and yet you relate to what I talk about, then this is for you too.

My culture is rife with racism, sexism, pretty much any 'ism'. If you're a Wog, you know what I'm talking about. In fact, it is so well known and talked about, that people have made careers out of joking about it, and we can all relate to Sooshi Mango, Nick Giannopoulos, Joe Avati, George Kapiniaris, Everybody Loves Raymond, etc. just to name a few.

Yes, I've laughed at their jokes and even attended some of their shows. Their satire is funny because it's bloody relatable! But at the back of my mind there's always a niggling voice that says, 'OK, but this is actually our lives ... are we ok with this? This needs to change ... why isn't it changing?!'

As a woman growing up in this culture, it feels oppressive as much as it is supportive. I grew up being taught that women do not speak up, and that my role is to be a good wife and mother, who cooks and cleans and devotes her life to her family.

The men around me never cleaned up after themselves ... it was always the women in the kitchen. The unfairness of this weighed heavy on me, but I never said a word. I could write a whole book filled with sexist quotes from family members and the Wog community (I might just do that one day).

As if that wasn't enough to deal with as a young woman, there was the casual attitude towards abuse. Ask any Wog and they will tell you that, at the very least, they had an item (such as shoes or a wooden spoon) thrown at them, and most likely they were smacked by their parents.

It was so normal that no one batted an eyelid. Now, it's called abuse. Even today, in the Wog community, there is flat out denial that hitting is a form of physical abuse. And that's without mentioning the emotional and verbal abuse, designed to control children and keep the family 'close'. Its par for the course. All part of being 'Wog'.

We have generations of Wogs growing up thinking this behaviour is ok. That being treated with disrespect is ok. And even further, that we need to RESPECT the people that are abusing us.

Respect is big in the Wog culture, but it goes only one way. You respect anyone who is older than you, regardless of what they say or do. And if you are a child, you aren't worthy of any respect, and should be seen and not heard at all times.

Moving on to a lighter topic now ... racism. I simply cannot wrap my mind around the concept of immigrants hating other immigrants. What? Che cosa? Ti les re? We Wogs are ALL immigrants.

Yet, it is so normal to sit around a dinner table and talk about the 'bloody *insert current immigrant culture*' who are 'taking all our jobs'. I don't know how my family fail to see the hypocrisy.

Growing up, my family would ask me who I was hanging out with. I would be warned not to hang out with certain ethnicities, some of which were also considered Wogs! If that's not confusing for a child, I don't know what is.

Body autonomy and personal space was simply not a thing taught to us. Kissing each other on the cheek and hugging is how we say hello in Wog culture, regardless of whether we feel comfortable with it or not.

I remember hating kissing people I didn't know (and a few that I did when I got that 'icky' feeling), and yet mum would give me 'that look' and I'd suck it up and do what I was told. The issue with forced physical contact is that it teaches kids to question the messages their bodies are sending them, which becomes an issue around consent. On top of that, it breeds people pleasers who don't know how to say 'no'.

The weird thing is, being in the culture and surrounded by the same type of people ... it becomes hard to see the more problematic aspects because it all just seems 'normal'. Being controlled by fear, being yelled at and hit, the guilt trips, the blatant sexism...it becomes part of the wallpaper and it can seem like there is no other way to live.

It's only when I stepped outside of my comfort zone and started to experience different cultures and ways of life, that I began to see the generational cycles at play that are keeping my family from living their best lives. And once I saw them, I couldn't un-see them. Ignorance truly is bliss. And yet, I wouldn't un-see them if I could, because the 'seeing' has allowed me to heal and to choose how I want to live my life – as a free individual who deserves to be treated with dignity and respect.

This 'seeing' prompted me to parent my daughter in a way that is different to how I was parented. I am a 'Cycle-breaker' and its bloody hard. Like, so so hard!

I wrote the poems in this book as I was 'waking up' to the abuses of the Wog culture. Through the liberation of writing, I began to heal a lot of traumatic experiences from my childhood.

The book takes you on a journey through the emotions that are often experienced during healing. While it is set up in a linear way, going from emotions like anger and ending at higher vibrations, like love, I can assure you the healing journey is anything but linear – it's a jumble of moving from the 'higher vibration' emotions and then swinging back to fierce anger and rage. Such is the beauty of being a messy human with the courage to explore ranges of emotion as they arise.

To end, I am a proud feminist fighting within a culture that still tries to keep women silent and confined to the kitchen. If you identify with anything I have written, this collection of poems is for you. May you discover the lion within and, like me, find the courage to let out your ROAR.

Anger, Frustration, Hurt.

I wrote these poems after I had my daughter, when I finally opened my 'pandora's box', and began to properly process the trauma of my upbringing, and was feeling stuck in the generational cycles of my family.

GAME OVER

I don't like you…
or so you say –
a great way to
divert attention away

from you.

We were talking about
what YOU did;
instead of owning up,
you hid

behind me.

To make ME the villain
of this story,
and give yourself,
all the glory

is your tactic.

You act like such a
'strong' man,
Yet you can't handle it
When a woman

stands up to you.

You love
To cause fear
In the people
You are near …

for control.

So be it, if I must be seen
As the bitch.
As long as
I cause a glitch

in your game –

GAME OVER.

Once burned, twice shy

If I burn my feet
in your fire,
don't blame me
for seeking refuge
in cool waters.

Unsafe

The way you overpower
until we all cower,
as if you are superior
and we the plebs, inferior.

When you raise your voice
you give me no choice,
I simply can't stand by
when a child needs an ally.

Even though my hands are shaking
and my voice is close to breaking,
I call you out on your shitty behaviour.
(As a child, I wished for such a saviour.)

When you're around, an alarm is raised
your family, I've never heard praised.
My body tells me you're unsafe,
this time I'm listening to my heart's race.

Arm's length is where I'll keep you
if it was up to me, we'd be through,
but close I'll stay, for my daughter's sake.
There's just too much at stake.

Thank-you

After more than a decade of
bowing down
playing by
your rules,

I asked for one
small thing
that meant so much
to me.

You rolled your eyes
and did what you wanted –
Disregarded my feelings
like I didn't matter.

So, don't ever wonder
where the 'good girl' went.
You chewed her up
and spat her out.

For that I thank you.
I set fire to my remains
and like a phoenix
rose again:

I wouldn't fuck with the new version if I were you.

Chasey

I don't want
to see you
anymore,

yet,
here you are
at my door.

I hide away
until it's
safe,

waiting
for my narrow
escape.

It seems this is how
it's meant
to be.

I run away,
and then
you chase me.

Whatever I Want

"What is she going to do now?"

"What will she say?"

Whatever the fuck I want, OK?!

If that makes you uncomfortable,

Or if it's too real …

Feel free to avoid me,

For I'll never again kneel.

Injustice

The day you punished me
for something she did,
taught me that I was responsible
for the actions of others.
My cries of protest were silenced,
so, I became silent.

I can still remember
the anger boiling
my blood.
A deep sense of injustice
having been committed.
I wonder if you even
recall that day at all?

I know all parents
are imperfect.
But I'm pretty sure
slapping a child's cheek with such force
that their body reels sideways
is abuse.

In the end
I never stopped loving you.
it would take
an apocalypse
for me to cut you out
of my life.
But I guess a little validation
that what you did was wrong
wouldn't hurt.

Hypocrisy

You laugh
like it's a joke
pretending not to
notice the hate you just spoke.

You say
'they' are everywhere
taking our jobs
and it isn't fair.

Have you forgotten?
Just one generation past
we were the immigrants
does your memory not last?

It was us
who were taking the jobs
who had all the businesses
who were seen as mobs.

'Wogs' they called us
put us down
made us feel shame
and unwelcome in this town.

I simply don't understand
why empathy is not what you feel,
I'm just trying
to keep it real.

They also came here
seeking a better life
or simply to
escape strife.

So, when you sneer
with your nose in the air,
such hypocrisy,
how can you see it as fair?

Keep your racist remarks
to yourself
they belong,
on the shelf.

Rules of the game

Their heated gaze
feels like an unwanted caress.

'Why do you hate men?' he asks.
Apparently, to not want to be constantly sexualised is to hate men.

It's not men I hate,
it's the idea that they are owed the pleasure of feasting on my body.

There is a difference between desired attention
and unwanted attention.

For those who need clarification, it's simple:

If a woman looks uncomfortable,
avert your eyes. Respect her space.

If she is staring right back with flirty intention,
enjoy the game. She's an equal player.

Women need men to understand
the uneven power dynamics of this kind of exchange.

When a woman isn't into it? She's not cold.
She's not a bitch. She's simply not interested.

No one is automatically entitled to another human being's body,
including touching AND staring.
Let's re-write the rules of the game …
Consent extends to eye fucking.

What women face when they chase their dreams …

"I'd prefer it if you stopped the business … you'd have more time," he said.

More time for 'serving him and the household' is what he meant.

Feigned Ignorance

I see you
feigning ignorance,
pretending,
playing dumb,

I see you.
I know you see me too,
so, let's call it what it is …
Stop this damn charade.

I can't do fake smiles
forced conversations
acting as if everything is ok,
everything is not ok
so why pretend?

Let's speak our truths
let it flow
meet each other
where we're at,

even if we don't agree
or it ends worse than before,
anything is better than pretending.

Unwanted Admiration

See these breasts?
They fed my child,
a grander purpose
than a place for your eyes.

Notice my lips?
Aren't they so full?
Perfect for
caressing my child's cheek.

Don't even get me started
on my hips,
so wide
until my waist dips –
They helped me carry a pregnancy.

Enjoying your view of my ass
so full?
Think it's just for you?
What shit are you trying to pull?

My body is not
your wonderland.
The way you're assuming it's all for you,
it's a WONDER you LAND any girls at all.

Sexualisation

They sexualised me
from age thirteen.

'See you in 5 years,' he said,
marking his territory.

I looked down
face flaming with embarrassment,

begging for the ground to swallow me whole.
When I looked up

I saw Mum's eyes
so proud,

her daughter was getting noticed by men.

Silenced

When other women speak out,
you cheer.
When their honesty shines through,
it appeals to you.

You see them,
as strong women.
When I do the same,
I'm rude and at blame.

Perhaps it was me who trained you
to see me this way.
Kept my lips sealed for too long,
now everything I say sounds wrong.

You would rather keep me silent.
BUT ... I will be silenced no more.

More Than a Body

'Have you lost weight?'
'You're looking good.'

How was I looking before?
is my only real value in my appearance?

I know you mean it as a compliment.
But to focus solely on my body is to ignore
everything else I am.

My kindness.
My intelligence.
My wisdom.
My humour.
My strength.
My love.
My honesty.
My sharp wit.

All of it gets lost in how I appear to your eyes.
What about how I appear to your soul?

Can you not see beyond my body?

Invisible

Around people
he forgets
I exist.

I escape
to the bar:
numb me.

I return –
'Surprise!'

He didn't even
realise
I was gone.

Family Bonds

Invisible shackles
bind our wrists.

Impossible standards
on their lists.

Unspoken words
swept under the rug.

Open wounds
no one can plug.

Reflections of a Feminist

It intrigues me when they mock our pain,
as if they weren't the ones who gave it to us.

How they tell us we are 'overreacting',
as if we hadn't witnessed them put holes in walls.

('She must be on her period' ... ha, well what's your excuse then?)

How quick they are to remind us of who paid for it all.
They must have forgotten it was them who denied us the promotion,
who kept us in the kitchen.

How they warn us not to wear revealing clothes or walk by ourselves at night,
as if it's not them who assault and rape us.

And yes ...
We know it's not ALL men.

But it does affect ALL women.

So, if you identify as one of the 'good' ones ...
Ask yourself, 'what have I done to help?'

Rage

Bubbling under the surface,
molten lava inside.

Red hot rage.

We borrowed most of it
from those that came before.

Red hot rage.

For every time they were silenced
hurt with words, or fists … it grew.

Red hot rage.

It's time to let it free,
never again will we hide.

Red hot rage.

The world is ready
to spill forth the truth and honour them.

Red hot rage explodes and washes over all.

From the charred remains
new life begins to form,
hope springs anew.

Hurt

A hurt soul lashes out
like a wounded animal
protecting its home …
Trying to preserve the remains.

Fake Apologies

'I'm sorry you feel that way,'

Is how

they avoid

all responsibility

for their part

in why you

feel that way.

Refuge

when family is not
a safe place,

you seek refuge
elsewhere –

sometimes water
is thicker than blood.

Approval

I kept seeking approval
in the wrong places.
Asking those who hate their own lives
to bless me with acceptance,
as if their decree held any weight.

Expectations

One says, 'jump!'
The other says, 'skip!'
Here's me doing both,
trying not to trip.

The torture of insomnia

Work in the morning
A million things to do
Responsibilities you can't escape
Still, sleep alludes you.

Feminism

I bear witness to a woman,
as jaded and enraged as I,
let her roar out into the sky.

A sister reached out to embrace me,
she knows the uphill battle I'm facing.

I keep on pushing, I'm not quitting now …
Not when, collectively, we are ready to howl.

I see the tides begin to turn,
dissatisfaction with the status quo is the first step … baby let it burn.

I speak up, finally, to let it be known:

my decisions,

my words,

my actions,

are my OWN!

Things I was told growing up that would make me a slut

Tank tops.
Nail polish.
Skirts.
Heels.
Make up.
Long hair.
Lip gloss.
Jewellery.
Too much eye contact.
Being myself.

Generational Abuse

how can you show kindness
when all you've known is hardness?

how can you be vulnerable
when crying is akin to stripping yourself naked and dancing in the street?

the cycle can (and must) be broken
how? because I decide it is so ...
and so, it is

his father hit him
he hit me
i refuse to hit her

it ends with me

Insomnia

A tsunami of thoughts pinions me to the bed,
the weight crushing my chest.
All I pray for is a little rest

4 hours until morning …

I can hear the blood pumping though my veins,
each beat making me more insane,

3 hours until morning …

Sudden panic grips me
an endless list of unfinished tasks hits me,

2 hours until morning …

Sweating
every decision I am regretting,

1 hour until morning …

How am I going to make it through the day?
Will the baby be OK?

…

On and on the mind game plays
until the sun shines its first rays.

Welcome to 2022

It may have been funny in '78
but now it looks like you're spreading hate

Sexist? Racist? All of the above
as the Black-Eyed-Peas sang, 'Where is the love?'

Do you truly believe in the words you're saying?
Or is it just some sick game you're playing?

No one is laughing anymore ... you should be embarrassed
the thing is, nobody stands up to you, for fear of being harassed

I get it, they don't want to step on toes ...
Even if you've verbally punched them in the nose

But I can't let myself forget,
little ears are listening, little eyes are watching ...
If I say nothing, I fear I would regret

So, here goes ... leave it in '78
when the oppressed were silenced and the hair wasn't great

Hello, welcome to 2022
where everyone is accepted

Yes, even you.

The Parent Trap

Inside each other's pockets,
always with the latest gossip.
Unwritten, unspoken rules at play …
How are your children to know what's OK?
Taut is the hold on the chain,
how deeply they hide their pain.
Confused about whose thoughts are whose,
do they even know they can choose?
But wait, can one have a choice …
When one can't have a voice?
'Only the best' is what you wish … you say,
what is the price they must pay?
Grateful are they for your help,
never enough though, guilt must be felt.
That is how you keep them near,
their own lives away from you … is your greatest fear.

Anxiety

Itchy skin. Pounding heart. Dizziness. Confusion. Hard to breathe. Want to scream. Uncontrollable rush of thoughts. Alone. Overwhelmed. Overstimulated. Ashamed. Angry. Desperate for silence of the mind. Desperate for a break in thoughts. Craving affection, but don't you dare touch me. Tell me I'll be ok, only for me to call you a liar. Tell me I'm strong, only for me to disagree. Leave ... please don't leave me alone.

Dark Cloud

She hides her face
beneath the wide brim
of her black sun hat,
the way the sun hides its face
behind a dark cloud,
hidden but always there.
Ready to shine another day.

Hope, Strength, Healing.

I wrote these poems when I began the healing journey ... I'm not sure what came first, the writing of the poems or the healing. Maybe both at the same time.

This is where the mouse became the lion ... I stepped into my power and started speaking up for myself and what I believe in.

Soul GPS

If you lose yourself,
don't worry.

Your soul has a GPS.

It will always
find its way
home.

Moon Woman

She's like the moon,
with her endless cycles.

Sometimes there's a fullness to her,
and she overflows.

Other times she'll
hide from show.

She comes and goes,

pulls the tides
towards her,

and away again.

Stardust

Remind them
you are made of
stardust.

You shine
so brightly,
they combust.

Bow Down

She owns her bad-bitch energy
That shit is gold –
She knows
She can never be told

She's a grown woman now
Slaying her life –
She's not just
His little wife

She may have the ring
But don't ever forget –
She'd be just as successful
Had they not met

She's earned the throne
Show some respect –
Even if you struggle
To accept

Like her or hate her
She still wears the crown –
All of you haters
Can bow the fuck down

(Inspired by Beyonce)

Decisions

When you realise

you can decide to do

anything you want,

your life changes.

Magical

You, my love, can do anything.

Just because you have forgotten your power,

doesn't make you any less magical.

Watched

Eyes are always watching,
        green from envy
                lusty pink,
                      fire red full of judgement
    following my every move.

There was a time
        when I made every decision
                based on those Eyes
                    their opinions,
                    their expectations.

Now
    I look in the mirror
        at the only set of Eyes that matter
                and I know the way,

they still watch …
                        I no longer care.

Alive

The stinging cold
feeds my soul.
Every cell
awakening from its slumber,
the most alive
I've felt in years.

Recovering People Pleaser

At People Pleasers Anonymous,
we tell stories of how we have overcome
the need to live for others' approval.

Each 'no' receives a standing O,
each boundary created, a hallelujah
to finally live free of others' expectations.

To be OK being seen as the villain,
as long as you are your own hero,
deserves celebration and fanfare.

Energy

Energy
tingling in my veins,
pulsing in my ears,
static in my head,
vibration in high frequency.

Slow
slow
slow
it down.

Throw off the extra energy
it was never mine to keep,

the balance returns.

Awakening

It feels as if women all over the world have had a collective awakening.
Or maybe, it's just we have all had enough of patriarchy at the same time?

It's as if we are uttering a collective 'Fuck This'
Can you feel the power in #metoo?

Body Map

My body is a map,

               each scar,

                             a landmark

                                          of storms

weathered.

Take Up Space

Take up space
fill the room,
let them see you
in full bloom.

Springtime is here
you've arrived,
now it's time
for you to thrive.

Spread that sunshine
shine your light,
this has always
been your right.

Wild

To all the women,
who got told
they were

too opinionated
too loud
too much,

you were always
a wolf
among sheep.

Find your pack
and
run wild,

as nature intended.

Opinionated Woman

You tell me
I'm 'too opinionated'
as if I haven't heard you
comment on every decision I've ever made.

I embarrass you
in front of your friends;
Is it because you're afraid
they'll think you can't control me?
As if I'm a show dog
that refuses to perform.

'You make everyone uncomfortable', you say.
I think, you're just uncomfortable
around liberated women.

You're used to seeing
meek and
oppressed
women.

I am not that.
I will never be that.
If that's what you want
you know how to locate the door,

because I am a woman
who can't be contained.
My thoughts spill out of me,
I'm overflowing,

I'm too big
for your small room,
I need acres
to roam free,

I am who I am,
embrace it all,
love the overflow
or leave,

either way
I remain me.

I can spend my cash how I want

The next time
a man comments
on how much you spend
on fashion,

remind him
that you paid for it
with every penny
you earned.

Remind him
that women
no longer depend
on men, financially.

It's time
men stopped joking
as if it's
still the '50's.

Remind him
you don't need
his money,
you have your own.

You need no permission
so, ask for none,
You owe no explanation
so, provide none.

On acceptance of others

I accept a snake
for what it is,
I don't attempt to
change its nature,
I simply remove myself
from the reach
of its poison.

A conversation with my younger self

If I could talk to my younger self
I would go back to the day when
he pulled me up the stairs by my hair –
Told me to "cover up"

I'd tell 15-year-old me that
she did nothing wrong,
her body is not shameful,
is not a secret to be kept hidden –
It's them that need to learn
how to respect it.

I'd take her hand
we would face him together –
We'd giggle at his shocked look
when we refused to hide anymore,

I'd look into her eyes,
remind her she is not the mouse
that's what they want her to believe –
She's the fucking LION
don't be afraid to ROAR, my sweet.

I'd tell her not to worry
it won't always be like this,
one day
you will come to a fork
that forces you to choose
yourself or them –
You will choose YOU.

I'd acknowledge that
right now, her world
seems blue,
lonely –
The rainbow will return, my love
for now, stay strong.

I'd give her a hundred and one reasons
why, she is sunshine on a rainy day
why, what they say
doesn't matter anyway.
I'd explain to her
she is water
in its pure elemental form,
flowing,
fluid.
Quenching the throats of many –
Those that don't deserve the refreshment,
can choke on it.

I'd tell her the story
about the butterfly
who began life as a caterpillar,
lost under the giants' feet
until one day
she could fly above their heads.

I'd also admit
that while she will soar,
occasionally, a cloud will block the sun.
Her world will once again
fade to blue –
This time though
she will know what to do,

because
along her journey
she will find the gem hidden within,
her wisdom
her knowing
her Soul
and she will listen deeply –
It knows the way.

I'd embrace her
this young, scared, girl
"be wild and free", I'd whisper in her ear
no need to watch the clock
year after year.
For all this and more is coming to you,
no need to rush.
Embrace every challenge –
and celebrate every dream you crush.

The crazy one

You know you're onto something when they label you 'the crazy one' attempting to discredit you, so they can maintain their illusions.

Ignorance is only bliss for those that control the narrative, for those that benefit from the status quo.

When you challenge that, you are shaking the foundation their whole world is built upon, so they call you names.

Try to intimidate you.
Spread a false rumour or two.

At the root of it all is their fear.
Keep going.

Keep telling your version of the truth.
Keep peeling back the layers.

Who wants to be normal anyway?!

What trauma looks like to me

The crack in the armour,
the tear in the seam.
Not everything is
as it seems.
Trauma does that,
it hides away.
It comes out when triggered,
the way my legs tremble and sway.

This world that we live in,
can't handle our pain
our collective voices … the strain.
The patriarchy protects
those in power,
those without,
aren't allowed to flower.

Fear is the tool used to suppress,
to control a whole gender
keep us in distress.
I was afraid to look men in the eye,
I wasn't their equal,
so why even try?

Men, a superior sex
or so I was taught,
who deserved to be served,
without question or thought.
It was us who needed to manage
what we wore,
for fear of awaking the beast
and being labelled a whore.

The crack in the armour
will always remain.
But for now, at least,
some beasts have been slain.
We can show our faces, at last,
I hope the oppression can stay in the past.

Our cracks are how
the light gets in.
We earned our wings,
we won't let them win.

(Special thanks to Rupi Kaur for the writing prompt in her book, 'Healing Through Words')

Ignored

My voice was never heard.
I think it was because I was saying what people didn't want to hear.
What people weren't ready to face.
I learnt to distrust my voice. To question my instincts.

'It's not polite to ask so many questions,' people said,
'curiosity killed the cat,' the same people said.

That just made me wonder what the cat was looking at …
What was it willing to die for?
What was I willing to die for?
More importantly, what was I willing to live for?

I decided my voice is too important to be silenced.
I decided I am willing to live to speak my truth.

Breaking Cycles

My ancestors must not have had enough.
They must have known real hunger and starvation.
This fear of not knowing when their next meal would be was passed down through blood.
'Eat more,' they'd plead. I never ate enough.
I remember being chased around with food as a child,
the 6 or 7 meals made for me; I refused one after the other.
All the dishes set out in front of me.
A procession line of rejected food.
The desperation on their faces.
My deep desire to be left alone.
To exercise choice over what went in my mouth.
This childhood experience has translated into a sensitivity, a wound, around food.
I flinch whenever I feel pressured to eat.
I visibly recoil.
I want to run.
I try so hard to break this cycle for my daughter.
It's not easy.
My instinct is to do what was done to me.
To force. To chase.
It takes everything in me to bite my tongue. To sit on my hands when my daughter is at the dinner table.
And yet I can only control so much.
I can't control them. Those that are still stuck in the cycle.
I must navigate my own trauma being triggered, plus the emotional reactions of others, while making different choices for her.
I know it's worth it.
This is the loneliness of the cycle breaker.
This is the significance of the cycle breaker.

Liquid Gold

I believe we are liquid Gold,
poured into our body mould.

The power of silence

The wind on my face
the sun on my skin,
my feet on the Earth
my soul within.

Things I notice
when I am still,
doing nothing at all,
when I just chill.

In this space
my heart opens to me,
messages from my soul
laid bare to receive.

Honouring my knowing

That feeling when you know people are talking about you.
Your 'knowing' tells you the words are unkind and bitter.
You feel their black energy sizzling between you.
They don't need to say it to your face.
You have a 'knowing'
and you FINALLY choose to trust it.

You finally begin to trust your body when your heart jumps into your throat each time you are around them.
When your hands begin to shake.
Your legs feel weak.
This is all a message from your body.
THIS. PERSON. IS. NOT. SAFE!
You want to run.
And you would ...
But what happens when circumstances are such that you see this person regularly?
What happens when they are a part of your world?
What happens when it's not as simple as choosing to run?

I grew up knowing nothing about personal boundaries.
I ignored my body's messages.
Overbearing was normal for me.
If I dared to utter the word "no" I was quickly put back in my place.
As an adult, I accepted far more than I ever should have.
I smiled and nodded politely,
while inside I was screaming.

I accepted my place on the bottom of my cultural food chain.
That it was my job to be accommodating and silent.
While those "higher up" could do whatever the fuck they wanted.
I felt this injustice deep in my bones.
My blood boiled with unleashed rage.
Yet, I accepted it was my lot in life.

I know now this is called 'cultural conditioning'.
My upbringing installed software in my brain that kept me shackled to this food chain.
Until,
I broke free.

I un-learned and un-became.
That's when I discovered personal boundaries.
Now I know that freedom is my fucking birthright.
Now I know I can CHOOSE.
I CHOOSE to limit my time with these people.
I CHOOSE not to cut them out of my life completely;
I am not bitter
despite the way they treat me.
I harbour no ill-will.
I send them nothing but love
      from a distance.

Now, I listen to my body's messages.
I know how to protect my energy when I am in their presence.
I finally know how to honour my knowing.
How to honour me.

Belonging

You belong
in every room you inhabit.

No one
has the exact experiences you have.

You add value
by simply being.

It is safe
to take up space.

You belong.

Voices

We need every voice.
Don't discount yours just because they showed you it didn't matter.

You are not crazy.
You have every right to speak your truth,
even if your voice trembles,
even if your hands shake.

Your story matters.
We need every voice.

When a loved one is in an abusive relationship

It breaks them down little by little.

A put down here,
a slap there.

Intimidation,
a tool to control.
Slowly her world gets smaller.

You desperately want to help.
To get her out and remind her how FIERCE she is.
But, right now she's just a shell.

She stares at you with empty eyes,
glazed over, resigned.
She's frozen in place.

Trauma does that, I know now.
The anger and frustration were overwhelming.
Powerless ... losing her before my eyes.

When she was finally free,
he still had her trapped,
by the pain he had inflicted.

The healing is ongoing,
the invisible wounds cut deep.

All I can do is be there,
as she peels each layer bare.

My eyes filled with pride,
for this woman who has endured enough to want to forever hide.

Yet here she stands,
broken but whole.

A beautiful, tender, loving and FREE soul.

(To all women who have experienced abuse and those who have witnessed it ... you are warrior angels!)

His Actions

His actions are not my own.

Why does the woman always get the blame for the man's actions?
Instead of rallying together,
it becomes woman against woman.
The man lives on, untouched by the drama.
I get it, I am the easier target,
but my dear, I too am a victim.
Love will always be greater than hate,
together we can rise above the debate.

His actions are not my own.

The Controller

Do what you say.
At all times.
And then, we will get along just fine.

A puppet on a string.
I played my part.
Though not a single word was mine.

The act grew old;
my soul became weary,
the truth began to spill,
I opened my mouth,
for the very first time.

you didn't like it
I was misbehaving,
acting against the force of your will,
your precious status-quo
was challenged,
and with it the world you protected.

Never again,
will I stand on your line.

My voice is there for a reason.
Controller, you no longer control me.

I welcome this new season.

When Generations Collide

The old and the new
on the same family tree,
one side tradition
the other yearning to be free.

'Why don't they respect us?
We did what we were told
I can't believe they would be so bold!'
The traditionalists rage,
'So much is different in this day 'n' age.'

'Why can't they understand us?
All we want is acceptance
and the ability to choose
our own preference,'
The young one's cry,
who can't seem to do anything right, no matter how hard they try.

In the middle of this dance,
this push and pull,
are hearts of pure love, so full.

Can we meet there?
In the middle
where the ground is even?

We might not be able to see eye to eye,
but hearts don't have eyes,
and love doesn't keep score.

The old and the new,
together once more.

The Darkness Within

We lock them away,
hide them under the bed
pretend they don't exist.

shame,
anger,
jealousy,
desire,

Those parts of ourselves
they taught us to hate,
we repress
we deny.
They become our "Voldemort",
They shall not be named
yet they remain inside of us,
continuing to tear us apart from within.

I wonder what would happen if they saw the light of day?
Still troubled parts, still dark,
but loved anyway.

Walls

Brick by brick
I stacked them high,
making sure none could enter.

Alone in my fortress
protected from harm,
none could hurt my centre.

A lonely game
this became,
and I my own abuser,
the fortress now a prison cell,
my own creation turned to hell.

Brick by brick
I tore them down,
inviting them to enter.

Daily Renewal

Burn me from within
cleanse me of my sin,
pure fire in my soul
a knowing that unfolds
the blaze consumes all.
I answer the call
I am born anew
each day that's through,
tomorrow I will wake
to a new state.

Look Within

When you can't see ahead
look within,
when what's behind hurts
look within,
when chaos surrounds you
look within,
for within lies every answer.

Bewitched

They dance under the moon,
holding hands.
Chanting words others wouldn't understand.
Such a bewitching sight to see,
three sisters prancing beneath the trees.

Cut the cord

In your eyes,
is my life so linked to yours
that you can no longer tell the difference?

Is that why you feel
betrayed when I choose
to live a life that you feel
is out of your reach?

Or could it be a touch of envy
that curls your lip just so?

Is it that I have decided
to live the life
you have always pined for,
but fear kept you from?

Whatever your answers, my response is this:
I'm done shouldering your problems,
they were never mine anyway.

I'm cutting the cord.

You …

You …
Can.
You …
Must.
You …
Will.

It all starts
with you.

Sisterhood

A sister once told me,
'Enough is enough,
it's time we're no longer
harassed with this stuff.'

Stranger to myself

I haven't been alone with my thoughts in so long
I've forgotten how to talk to myself.
My accent has changed,
it has a little more edge to it now.
Like I've lived in a foreign country for too long.
I am a stranger in this country,
and yet I no longer belong at home.
I live in the in between,
searching for a comfortable place to rest my longing soul.

Universe

I am this body lying on the sand
I am the wind blowing through my hair
I am the sun kissing my skin
I am the waves crashing on the shore
I am the gulls soaring overhead
I am everything
I am the universe
The universe is me.

Ancestral Messages

Never was your voice allowed.
Respect, you were not endowed.

The anger grew and grew inside,
Until it was a flood.

Little did you realise,
You would pass this down through blood.

For I hear your howls of rage,
Ringing through my veins.
In my ears you scream,
'Do not let it happen again!'

How many generations of our women have wept?
Longing for the freedoms from which they were kept.

'I hear you,' I answer to the voices inside.
This generation will not be taught to hide.

Watch how the light flows out of me,
Illuminating a path for all to see.

As my daughter and I dance under the sun,
Echoed in my ears is cackling laughter and fun.

For we did it,
Together we broke the spell
For those to come.
Enjoy the freedom well!

The Real Me

Who am I?
Really?
Underneath all this fog?
I wear so many masks
I've forgotten who the Real Me is.
Will the Real Alana please stand up?
Yes.
You ... sitting in the back.
Who? Are? You?
Finally, I see her.
There she is,
She's returned!

Welcome home my love,
I've missed you.
I embrace her,
Kiss her on both cheeks.
'I'm sorry,' I say,
'It's been years since I've called upon you,
Not mere weeks.'
I relearn her,
Study her mind and her heart.
Until it all comes rushing back,
Like we were never apart.

'Who is this?' they say,
'We've not met her before,'
'What happened to the docile girl with her knees on the floor?'
'She's gone now,' I reply,
'This is who I was before,
Before I twisted and bent myself to fit through your door.'

I'm done
Being round when, really, I'm square.
Me, myself, and I are free now,
We would love you to still care …
The same way you did when I couldn't return your stare.

'Care … care?' they say with a snare,
'We'll only care if you sign here, there, and there.'
But I'm done now.
I've had my fill of your game.
I'm playing my own game now,
And the rules aren't the same.

So, I shed my skin,
I am reborn.
Alana 2.0.
I welcome all with hearts pure, kind, loving.

As for those who can't accept,
Enjoy the show.
The light can be blinding,
I know.

Bring sunglasses … this bitch is about to glow.

Freedom

Choice should not be a reward
Dangled like a carrot on a string,
Just out of reach.

Choice should be a birthright.
We owe nothing when we are born.

Our family nurtures us until we are able to nurture ourselves.
Then ... they should let us go.

A butterfly does not stay in its cocoon to please its family.
It flies,
It is free ...
And
So are we.

Love, Connection, Relationships.

This section is dedicated to love and connection… the reason why we are all here.

I write about my friends, my partner, lost loves, my daughter, and my parents; Everyone who has touched my soul.

Sister

You've been there
Through all the years.
All the boys.
All the tears.

You and I
Have both changed.
But one thing
Has always remained.

Our deep respect
For each other.
Sisters,
From a different mother.

It's an honour
To walk beside you.
To watch the amazing
Things you will do.

I love you, girl,
I hope you know.
Let's keep giving
Them a show.

Full

My arms are full,
As is my heart.
I ache when
We are apart.

What If?

I remember what it felt like
To feel the heat of your eyes on me.
To watch you laugh
At something silly I said.

I loved to make you laugh.

I often wonder
If you knew
What you meant to me.

It's funny how,
No matter the time that passes,
I still remember it all
Like it was yesterday.

Each word.
Each touch.
Each shared memory.

So close,
Yet so far.

So many 'what ifs?'
What if I didn't run away every time it got too real?
What if I wasn't scared of rejection?
What if I kissed you?
Would you have kissed me back?
If I met you under different circumstances,
Would I still feel the same?

I have so many questions
That will never be answered.
This must be what
Regret feels like.

The thing that keeps me going
Is the belief that
Everything happens for a reason.

Maybe our story
Was meant to end there.
I just want you to know
I still care.

Dear Mama

Dear Mama,
One thing I need you to know
Is how fast I had to grow.
One thing I need you to hear
Is how, from you, I learnt to fear.
One thing I need you to say
Is that everything will be OK.
One secret I need to tell you
Before the years are through …

Did you know that, as a child,
I would sit in my bed at night,
Staring at all my toys,
Feeling wave after wave of guilt?
Tears would fall
Because I knew it all
Came from your hard work.
I knew how much you sacrificed.
I thought I didn't deserve
To have these things
At the expense of your happiness.

The force of love

We are each a channel of light –
Love is the material enabling us to shine bright.

Feel the energy bouncing between you and I –
We could bottle it and use it as fuel to fly.

Is that why those in power keep pushing hate?
Because they're afraid of the force love can create?

Stranger in my bed

Same eyes
That have looked into mine all of these years.
Same hands
That have touched every inch of my body.
Same lips
That have kissed mine thousands of times.
Yet,
You are a stranger in my bed.

Lying side by side,
Close enough to touch,
Yet neither one reaches out.
Might as well be miles apart.
How do we bridge this divide, my love?

I am still learning this new version of me.
She has not yet been acquainted with you.
The shyness, the awkwardness, the not knowing how to proceed.

Can we start again?
Learn each other as if new lovers?
'Hi, nice to meet you, my love …'

Parental Tension of Opposites

Slow down and stay my baby forever …
Hurry up and get through this tough developmental stage.

You are the cutest thing I've ever seen …
I swear you are the devil in disguise.

You anticipate what's next and love to be helpful …
When it doesn't suit you, then it's a battle of the wills.

Your hugs and kisses are so sweet …
Your hits and snubs cut me so deep.

I want to spend every minute with you …
I want to run away and be left alone.

You teach me patience and a love so deep …
You trigger every nerve in my body.

To My Daughter

Honey muffin, cherry blossom, boo …
These are some of the names I call you.

Never have I met a heart so pure,
You've been here before. Of this, I'm sure.

Your laughter, your joy, are infectious to everyone you greet,
They say never have they met anyone so sweet …

Balanced, of course, by a stubborn mind, so fierce,
You convey so much with that one look; you pierce.

Keep your fire, my love, it will serve you well.
To all those who judge you, I've no doubt you'll say, 'go to hell.'

You are a free spirit, born to dance under the sun.
Keep being YOU, live life, and above all … have FUN!

Motherhood

They say it's like having your heart outside of your chest,
I think that really explains it best.

I'll admit no job is as all-encompassing,
You give it your all and still feel something missing.

Nothing can beat the feeling of their head on your shoulder,
Wanting to slow time before they get older.

You want to cherish each giggle, each hug, each wet kiss …
These, you know, will be the moments you miss.

You know deep down the day will come, and all too fast …
When this piece of your heart ventures out to explore the world so vast.

Though you know you will encourage them to live big and push past fears,
It will take everything to hold back your own tears.

Though I am at the beginning of this journey,
About motherhood one thing is clear …
No matter the years or the distance apart,
My love won't ever disappear.

Bluebird

My bluebird, I know you are flying free …
Your spirit is forever a part of me.

We existed in one body for a time.
You were not meant to remain mine.

You kissed my womb to teach me a lesson –
Always savour every single blessing.

For how much more blessed can I be,
to have a bluebird forever watching over me?

Tina/Mothers of immigrants

You sent your son across the sea
To a place you knew you would never see.

Seventeen, and on a boat to a new land,
He set out to create a life by his own hand.

How your heart would have squeezed in your chest,
Without knowing he was safe, you could not rest.

My dear, your sacrifice was not in vain.
Look how much your people have gained.

It is you we thank for this life we live …
Your son, to us you did give.

I feel you both, reunited at last.
Your souls so near, though now you've passed.

Gratitude and love I send to you,
For watching over my journey, the whole way through.

Single Parents

I am in awe of
Single parents.

You are angels.

Mama,
I don't know how you did it.

With such humility,
Such grace.

To shoulder that much responsibility,
Alone …

All single parents
Deserve a throne.

What I'm going to teach my daughter …

- It's her choice who touches her body (including hugs and kisses from family),
- As an adult, she can do whatever she wants with her life, no matter what other people say (including me),
- I am not her responsibility,
- She owes me nothing,
- Honesty is not rudeness,
- Speaking up for yourself is not impolite,
- When people remind you what they've done for you, it's manipulation,
- It's ok (even healthy) to disagree,
- Her voice matters,
- A partner should see her as an equal,
- She deserves respect from every human being, and if she doesn't get it then that person is not worth her time or energy.

Pure Love

God.
Buddha.
Allah.
Universe.
All of the above.
It doesn't matter which you follow,
The essence of all is Pure Love.

Naked

It is a beautiful thing to feel you can be yourself with another.
To fully disrobe and be gloriously naked in their presence.

The mask that normally remains bound to your face can finally untie and sit on the shelf.
The polite pants and the trivial talk t-shirt can be shed, too.

The undergarments that hide our true nature can slip down our legs.
Until …

There … we are.

Our truest self.
Our higher being.

Oh, what a feeling to be naked in your presence.

Thoughts, Opinions, Learnings.

The inner workings of my mind …

Impact

Sometimes I stop
And think about
All of the people
I've known
In my life
And I wonder
Whether they
Think about me.

We can never know the impact we have had on other peoples' lives
…

Judgement

You'll be judged
No matter what you do.

You might as well
Do what you want to.

My Perfect Day

Window open.

                Cruising down a new road.

                                Music blaring.

Singing the high notes.

                Taking in the beautiful scenery.

                                It's as close to heaven as
                                I'll ever be.

R.E.S.P.E.C.T (what it means to me)

Every soul deserves
To be shown
RESPECT.

Regardless of their:
Age
Race
Gender.

Respect is not
Hierarchical.
It is reciprocal.

I will not
Automatically
Show you deference
Simply because you
Are older than me.

Who can know
The number of lives
Our souls have lived?

A child has
As much wisdom
As an elderly person.

If given the chance to speak it.

Question

Have you noticed that when you decide to distance yourself from toxic people and no longer react to their games,

They pursue you more aggressively, doing everything they can to get a reaction from you?

Hypothesis

My hypothesis is this …
People who say,
'How could they do that?'
Are actually saying,
'I wish I could do that.'

What I Keep Hidden

The past often visits me
When I least expect it:
Past trauma
Past loves
Past happy memories.

The past rushes over me like a waterfall.
I couldn't stop it if I tried,
It crashes through my brain
Freezing me in place
I am no longer here, but there.

The slightest thing can trigger it:
A smell
A noise
A word,
As if a magician has put me under his spell.

I am powerless to stop it
And so, I surrender,
I live it all over again,
Like a movie in my head,
Except this time, I choose the ending.

I wonder if others spend as much time in the past?

Autumn Leaves

Fall and float down,
Congregate on the ground,
A pile of bronze celebrating their maturity.
'Remember when we were young and green?' they reminisce.
Alas, there is a special privilege that comes with their bronze hue,
A spring full of growth and new beginnings,
A summer of living under the sun,
A lifetime well lived,
A place on the pile, their badge of honour.

Bitter People

Some people are
Just waiting for
You to fall.

It is the only way
They know how to
Make themselves feel better.

Some people hate their life
and want others to join their pity party.

Misery loves company,
Or so they say.

To these people
Show kindness
But, protect your space.

Their energy is infectious

Thank you – from my heart to yours – for connecting with me through my words.

My hope is that you've found some comfort in knowing you are not alone. I hope my words have stoked a fire within that empowers you to stand up for what you believe in.

Love is always the answer, but sometimes you need to melt the ice with your rage before you can get to the love frozen within. That is what I found, in any case. Writing these poems helped me to work through all of the rage I was feeling internally. I didn't have to say any of this to 'their' faces, it was enough to write it all out.

I wish you strength, love, and light on your journey.

About the Author

Salina is a poet, student, soul coach, healer, and mother.
When The Mouse Became the Lion is her first published book.